The 446th B

Who were the 4...

The 446th Bombardment Group was a part of the 20th Combat Wing, of the Second Air Division of the USAAF, which was itself a part of the USAAF Eighth Air Force. Although the 2nd Air Division was fundamentally Norfolk based, the Suffolk station of Flixton was integral to its story. The 446th were known as *'The Bungay Buckaroos'*.

During the turbulent days of World War II, Norfolk, Suffolk and the wider East Anglia became home to the Mighty Eighth Air Force as it took advantage of the relatively short flight time between the Norfolk coast and mainland Germany to get its war planes to Germany and back in the most advantageous manner. In the early part of this campaign, Flixton Airfield became home to the 446th Bomb Group, made up of the 704th, 705th, 706th and 707th Bombardment Squadrons. Station 125 as Flixton was known to the American military, was the home to over 2,800 men, at any one time, who flew and maintained the 446th's B24 Liberators that operated on an almost daily basis into the German heartland, to harass and damage the Nazi war machine as much and as often as possible.

The 446th were activated in America at Davis-Monthan Field near Tucson in Arizona and trained at Lowry Field, Denver, Colorado prior to their departure to Europe.
In early November 1943 they arrived at Flixton and took up residence in a barely finished airfield. Only a few weeks later on Dec 16th they were fully operational, flying combat missions in support of the war effort, and although they were not yet aware of it, they were already earmarked for the legendry 'Big Week' raids in February 1944, aimed to weaken German aircraft production.

This is how it looked to *'The Bungay Buckaroos'*, recorded on a day to day basis, by their own cameras.

Flixton's longest runway is North-East / South-West (05/23 - 2000yards) with the main technical site orientated to the top right of the photo. Oddly, the airfield's two T2 hangars are not on the same site. The two cross runways were the traditional 1400 yards long and mainly used for landing only, when the wind was not suitable for the 07 / 25 runway. All runways were the standard 50 yard width, and somewhat unusually, made from concrete, tarmac and wood chippings.

Flixton was just over six miles to the south west of the Suffolk town of Beccles, and close to the USAAF airfields of Hardwick and Seething. These three adjacent airfields formed the 20th Combat Wing. The small Suffolk market town of Bungay to the East, was the nearest centre of urban life, as Flixton was surrounded by a very rural environment, even for airfields traditionally located in fairly uninhabited farmland.

After hostilities ceased, the 446th went home and the RAF moved in for about ten years, moving out themselves in 1956. After a few years of neglect, the airfield became the focus for The Norfolk and Suffolk Aviation Museum, one of the regions premier museums dedicated to aviation history.

This is what the Bungay Buckaroos came to England to do…

…High above their adopted home of East Anglia, they formate together to take their bomb loads across to mainland Europe to confound the German war machine.

This is where all the real work went on, high in the sky over enemy held territory…

…There is over a year between the photos, but the job never varied.

This is what you all set out to do, every day…

…hammer the enemy and bring the war to an end as soon as possible.

Day in and day out you hounded the enemy positions, airfields, industrial plants and lines of communications…

…you were always going to win, it was just a question of how long it would take and how many of your buddies would not make it home.

HEADQUARTERS STATION #11
CARIBBEAN WING, ATC

Date 4 November 1943

PILOT :   2nd Lt Paul L. Park

AIRPLANE : B-24H   42-7612

1. Your final Destination is _____ United Kingdom _____

for assignment to _____ European Theatre of Operations _____

reporting upon arrival thereat to the Commanding General for further orders.

2. Crew members and/or Passengers assigned to the same Shipment or Flight Echelon, will be notified of Final Destination one (1) hour after take-off.

3. Should it be necessary to return to this station, secrecy of this movement will be maintained in accordance with AR 380-5.

By order of Colonel TRUESDELL:

MARION E. O'QUIN
1st Lt., Air Corps
Asst. For Opns Officer

And this is how it had all started…

…one day, just a few months ago, this guy from the Squadron Office had come up to you and the rest of the crew and handed you each a letter. It was Uncle Sam's invitation to head to England and put all your training into practice.

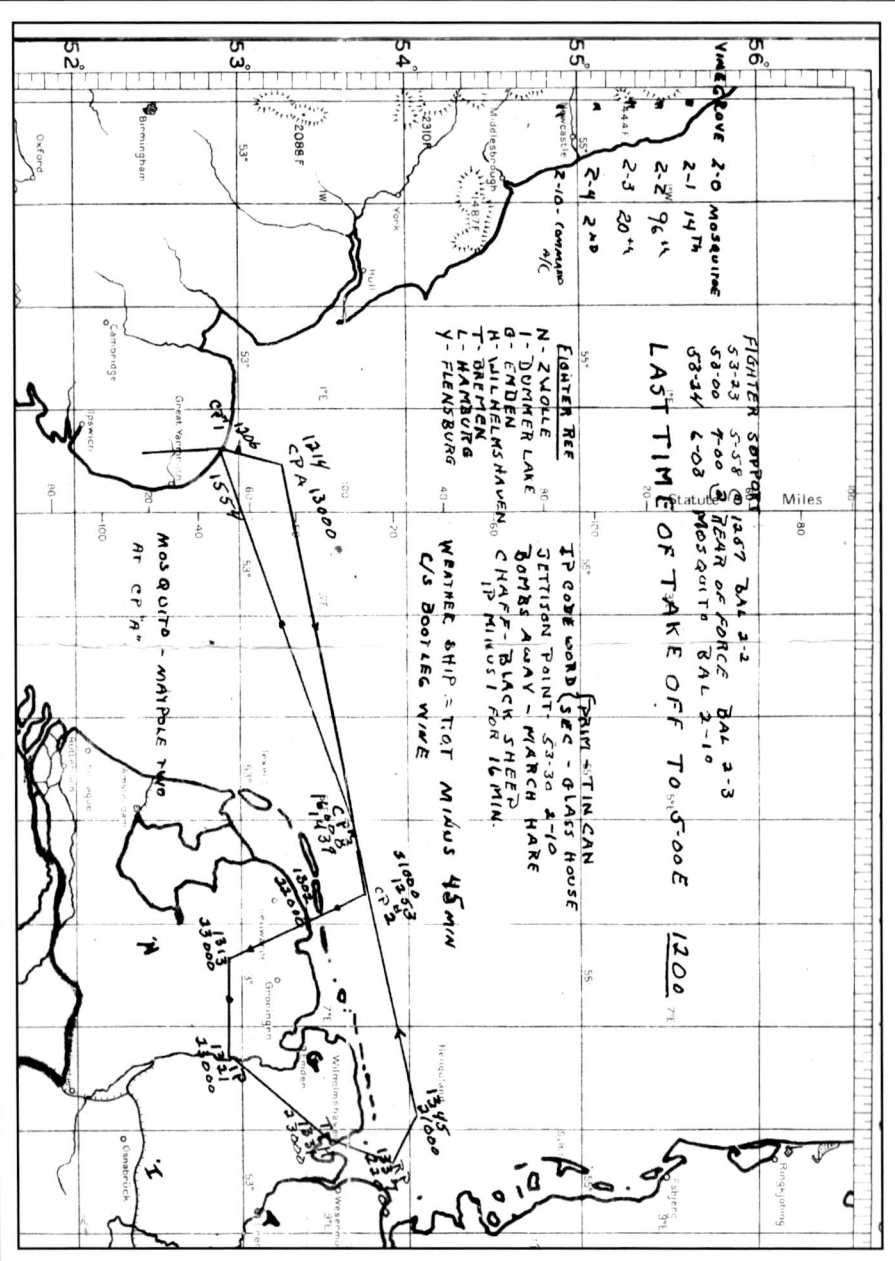

Then one day soon after arriving in England,
they handed you one of these…

…and your target for today is…

Before any raid there were always the briefings…

….you then did everything together. Taxi out to the take off point, then stick in formation as you headed towards today's target. It was always like that.

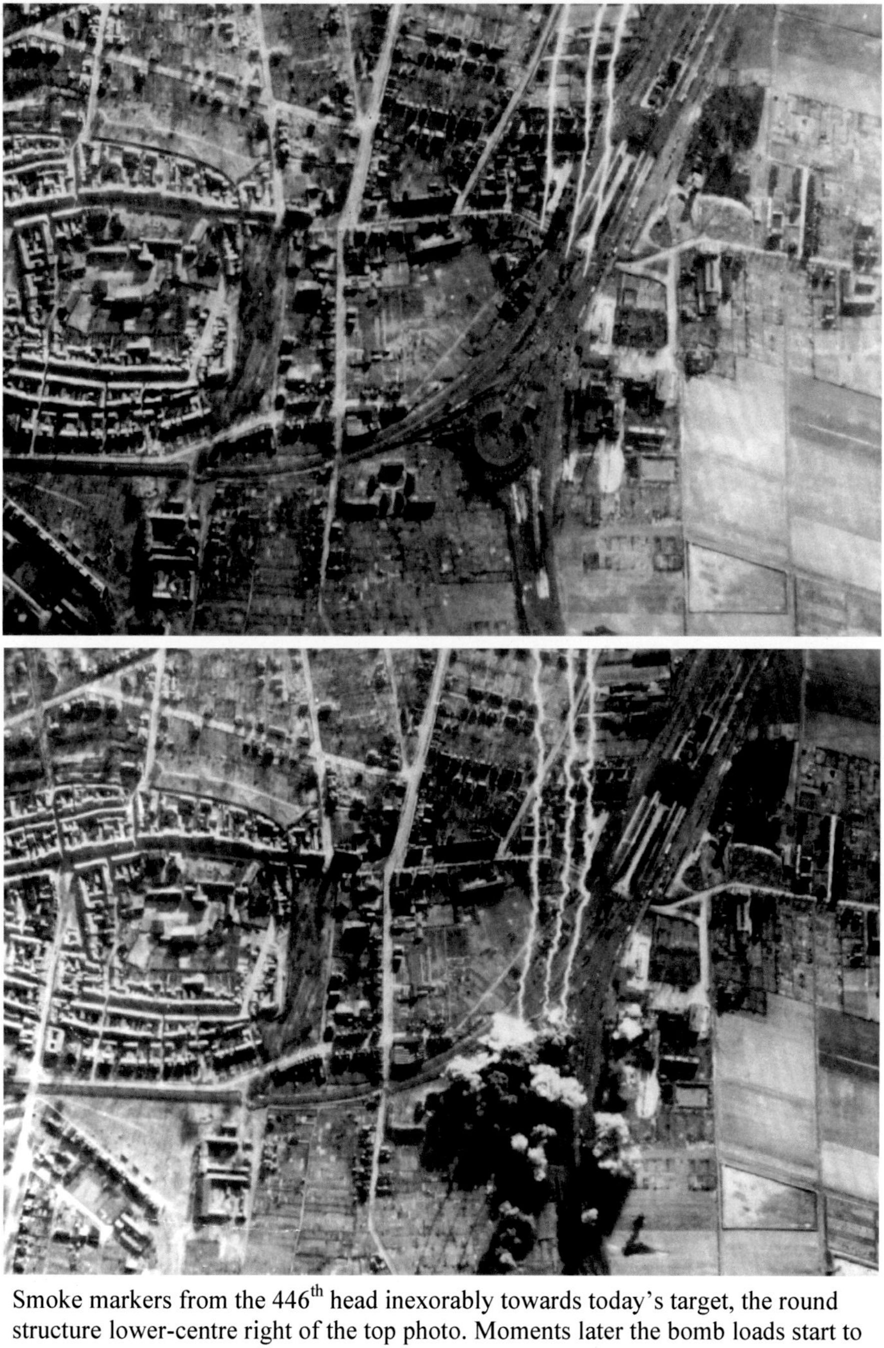

Smoke markers from the 446th head inexorably towards today's target, the round structure lower-centre right of the top photo. Moments later the bomb loads start to rain down after the markers. Job done.

On the next mission it was another part of the enemy war machine that received the full attention of the 446th's bombers' cargo.

This had been your cargo a few hours ago…

      …the guys in these pictures were your armourers from the Ordnance Section. A few hours before take off they had loaded the bombs in your plane, and prepared them for your own bombardier to deliver them to mainland Europe.

Even when the airfield's mud got into the act with the crane, these boys still made sure you got a full load of bombs for every mission.

They knew that the more bombs that hit their targets, the sooner the war would be over and the sooner they got to go home…

…that was uppermost in everyone's mind.

Once the mission started and the drone of the B-24s had faded away, all they had to do was wait, like everyone else, for their return. It was just not an easy time.

You could go back to your hut, sit around and read, write letters home or just hang around with the boys…whatever you did, you could not rest until 'your' planes got back safely.

But it did give you time to get a few things done…

…like a haircut…

…like getting a photo or two of you and your buddies to send home: It would help to set the folks minds at rest a little.

You also got a chance to look around the local countryside…
…and make friends with the girls working on the farms.

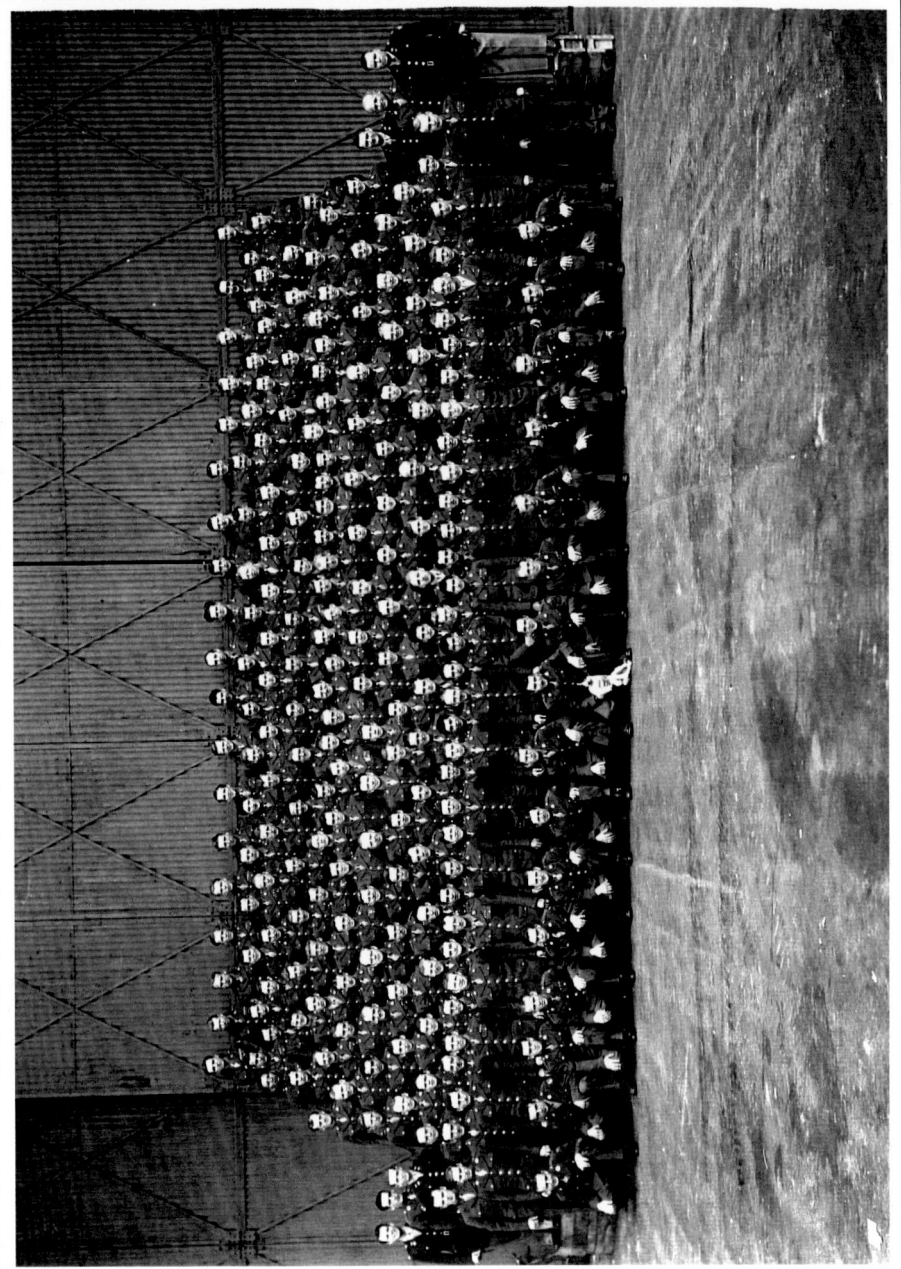

Then there were the official photos that were needed by the 'Big Brass'…
…these were the boys from the 460th sub-depot.

Visitors to the 446th

The P38 Lightning

The B17 Fortress

Then of course The RAF dropped in from time to time.

The Halifax

One misty day this RAF Stirling literally dropped in.

In reality its landing was more of an 'arrival', but you could see why from the damage it had sustained. It was lucky to have kept flying as long as it did.

Some of the B-24's of the 446th could also reduce themselves to scrap when the crews had a bad day…

…luck played a big part in every mission.

On this occasion when the 446th's Merle Lee skated to a stop at Hawkinge, in Kent, the plane was trashed, but the fuselage stayed intact. That was lucky.

When this B-24 of 707 Squadron crash landed on the airfield, it became an instant attraction to the local children…

…even the girls. Here Pat and Poppy Nunn (right) can be seen under the huge tail plane of the bomber.

This is where the men of the 446th lived, and these were some of the regular sights they saw around Flixton on a day to day basis…

…though it has to be said the days on which the gun crews could sunbathe were pretty few and far between.

The senior Group and Station Officers were often seen on the control tower looking skywards…

…the little armoured car was however, more of a rarity.

A guy working on an engine was a regular sight all across the base.

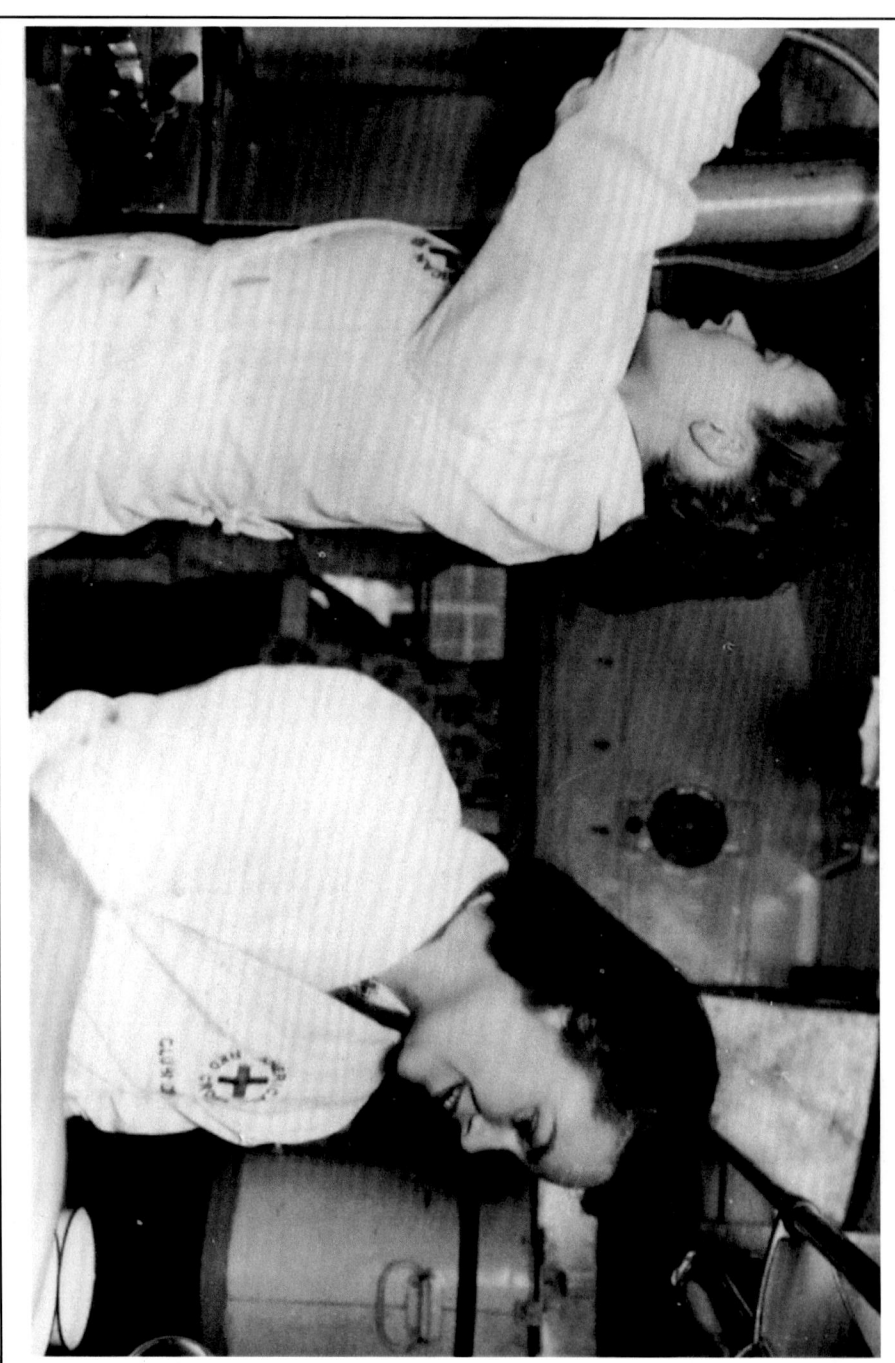

…as were the Red Cross girls. Thankfully!

On a station as big as Flixton, it always amazed the guys, how little space they got for themselves…

…anyway, you didn't always get much spare time to be there, I guess that was how the Big Brass saw it.

Nose art from the 446th Bomb Group.

Satan's Little Sister

Wistful Vista

And a piece of nose art on Old Faithful as far down the nose as you can get!

For sure the Consolidated B-24 was the most important mode of transport on the base…

…but the British built Raleigh bicycle came a pretty close second.

Whenever your buddy took a photo of you, or you took a photo of him, it always seemed that a bicycle, or at least part of it, appeared in the shot.

Even on a snowy day at the line hut, in the dead of winter, there were bicycles propped up either side.

Only occasionally did the mode of transport vary.

However, the B-24s always came first.

That applied whether you were wearing a nice clean pressed uniform in a squadron office…

…or old, oily fatigues, out on the line.

Sometimes you did not get out of your fatigues for days on end.

It was the same for everyone in all the ground crews of any of the squadrons of the 446th.

Sending wave after wave of fully loaded bombers into the enemy heartland and forcing an end to the war…that was the mission…

It never wavered.

The 446th at work…

This is how you liked to see 'your' B-24s.
High in formation heading off to Europe…

…then returning safely and undamaged at the end of
the mission. It didn't always work out like that.

All too often it ended like this.
Ball turret shot away. Ball Gunner MIA, presumed KIA.

In war, things rarely go to plan, and although the 446th's record was good amongst the Bomb Groups of the 2nd Air Division, there were many days like these…

…your buddies in the top plane made it back; by the time the lower photo was taken, there were already several empty places at the breakfast table…

The dangers for the 446th were still there, even within a few weeks of the war's end, as this superb John McCoy Jr., painting depicts.

The mission was Wesendorf. The date April 4th 1945.

Even supply drops were dangerous, and you never took them lightly…
…the easiest of mission still had the capacity to bite back.

For aircrews and
ground crews
alike, all
missions were
important…

…all missions
were a matter of
life and death.

For some aircrew of the 446th, it was OK one day then a dramatic change the next.

There was the sudden shock of being photographed one day by a friend, standing, smiling, between your two best buddies…

…Then the next thing you knew, a surly faced prison guard was also keen to take your photo.

He and his fellow Prisoner of War team were definitely not smiling.

They would soon explain their feelings on the war, your bombing and the Nazi view on the U.S. involvement in the war…

…Station 125 seemed a long way away.

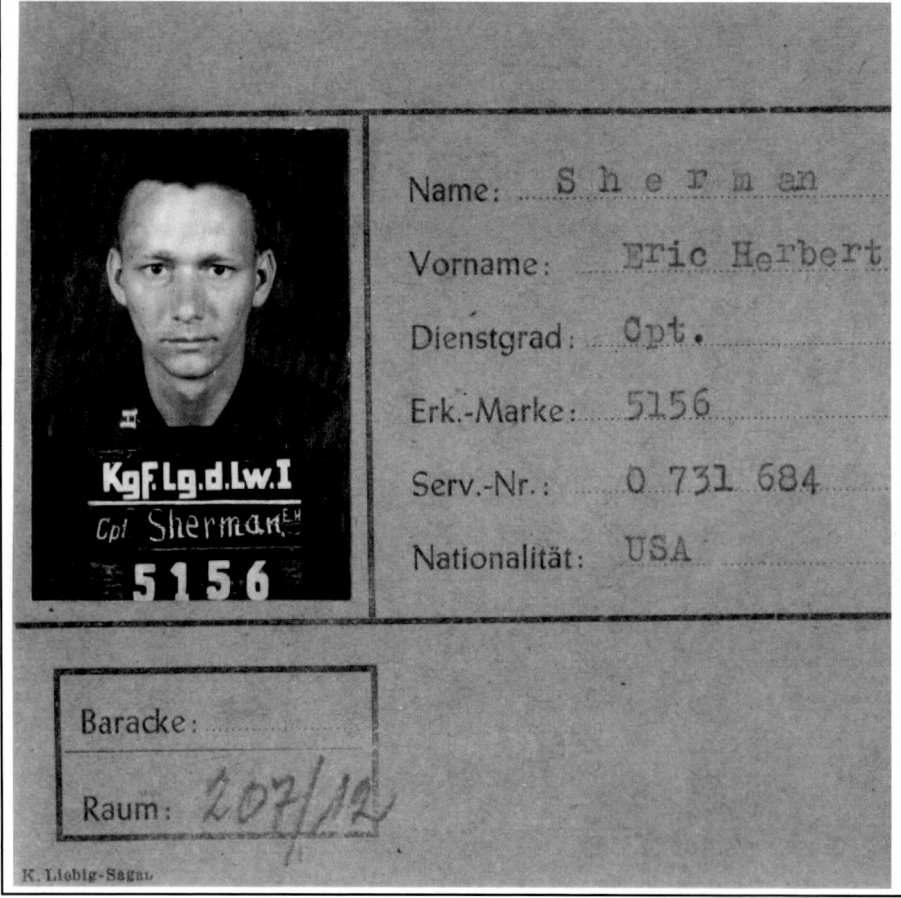

Name: S h e r m an

Vorname: Eric Herbert

Dienstgrad: Cpt.

Erk.-Marke: 5156

Serv.-Nr.:   O 731 684

Nationalität: USA

Baracke:

Raum: 207/12

K. Liebig-Sagan.

Someone back at an office at Flixton had the lousy job of letting your folks know that you were officially M.I.A. (Missing in Action).

It could take weeks or even months to get the information through that you were in fact still alive and a Prisoner of War.

Such was the pace of the war, that by the next mission was flown, there was a new crew drafted in to replace you.

It was not hard to understand, you had done the same thing yourself, just a year or two earlier.

More 446th Nose Art.

The Big Drip

Black M

"Tail Wind"…a popular theme amongst all 2nd AD aircrew.

Dragon Lady

Dinky Duck

Home Breaker

Lazy Lou

More Nose Art from the 446th…

…including Red Ass in flight.

Further Nose Art from the 446th.

Glamour and Humour again side by side on the airfield apron…

…Naughty Nan had 41 mission indicators to her credit…

…while Mighty Mouse had yet to break its duck, when this photo was taken.

UNITED STATES ARMY AIR FORCE 446th BOMB GROUP (H) STATION 125

446 BOMB GROUP

704 SQDN   705 SQDN   (H) AIRBASE CONCERNS   706 SQDN   707 SQDN

NOVEMBER 1943 TO JUNE 1945
273 COMBAT MISSIONS OVER 6000 PERSONNEL SERVED
456 KILLED IN ACTION, 66 AIRCRAFT LOST
THIS GROUP LED THE 8TH AIR FORCE ON THE FIRST MISSION OF D-DAY 6TH JUNE 1944

B-24 LIBERATOR

SUPPORT UNITS
DETACHMENT A 1248TH M.P. CO (AVN) · 460TH SUB-DEPOT CLASS I · 212TH FINANCE SECTION
558TH ARMY POSTAL UNIT · 589TH ARMY POSTAL UNIT · 2967TH FINANCE DETACHMENT
2038TH ENGINEER AVIATION FIRE-FIGHTING PLATOON · GROUP HQ AND HQ SQUADRON
260TH MEDICAL DISPENSARY AVN (R.S) · DETACHMENT A 885TH CHEMICAL COMPANY
25TH STATION COMPLEMENT SQUADRON (SP) · 639TH MATERIAL SQUADRON
214TH QM COMPANY SERVICE GROUP AVN (R.S) · 178TH AIR SERVICE GROUP
1821ST ORDNANCE SUPPLY & MAINTENANCE COMPANY (AVN)
815TH AIR ENGINEERING SQUADRON

REMEMBER THEM

The air crews of the 446 Bomb Group may never have thought of themselves as 'Young Eagles' when they took off on their missions, but they were! These young men, along with maintenance crews and other support personnel, many in their teen years, had eagerly answered their country's call, doing what they believed they had to do. The courage, stamina and honor displayed by these men can never be fully described. They carried the fight for freedom through the deadly skies over France, Germany, Belgium and Austria. They also brought their charm and enthusiasm for life to the inhabitants of East Anglia. Generous and outgoing, they in a short time, won the friendship of the English people among the many airbases and became affectionately known as the Bungay · Buckenoo at Flixtondrome

"In the words of Abraham Lincoln, 16th President of the United States of America
— The world will little note nor remember what we say here, but it can never forget what we did here."

58

There are two memorials to the 446th; one at the site of the old airfield, (left) and one at The Norfolk and Suffolk Aviation Museum (Half a mile to the North of the old airfield site) shown here to the right of the photo. Both are very well cared for and definitely worth a visit.

All photographs from or via the Alan Hague and Tony North collections.
Cover painting by John T. McCoy Jr., (446th Artist)
Centre painting by John Constable Reeve. (Museum Artist)
For further study, the authors recommend:-
                www.aviationmusdeum.net/446bg.htm
                www.446bg.com/opening.htm
                history446@aol.com

or read…   History of the 446th .G. (1946) Ed Castens
                    The 446th revisited (1998) Ed Castens
                    The History of the 446th B.G. (1989) H.E. Jansen
                    The History of the 446th Bomb Group (2003 reprint.) H.E. Jansen

Facts and Figures on the 448th

Arrived   16th Nov1943

Departed   5th July 1945

Aircraft Used   *Consolidated Liberator B24*
4 x 1,200 Pratt & Whitney Radial engines
10 man crew
Bomb load – 6 tons
All up weight – 29 tons
Top Speed – 290 MPH
Service Ceiling – 28,000 ft
Fuel Load – up to 3,516 gallons
Range – 2,100 miles

Bomb Group   *20th   Combat Wing (H)*

Complement   *446th Bombardment Group (H) Headquarters*
704th Bombardment Squadron (H)
705th Bombardment Squadron (H)
706th Bombardment Squadron (H)
707th Bombardment Squadron (H)
460th Sub Depot
1821st Ordnance Company
885th Chemical Company
1248th Military Police Company
2035th Engineer Fire Fighting Platoon
1214th Quartermaster Company
2967th Finance Section
260th Medical Company

Missions   *273 (7,259 Sorties)*

Ordnance dropped *16,818 Tons*

Losses 1943-1945   *Planes – 86*
Men – 456